SpringerBriefs in Criminology

Policing

Series Editors

M.R. Haberfeld
City University of New York
John Jay College of Criminal Justice
New York, NY, USA

More information about this series at http://www.springer.com/series/11179

Heath B. Grant

Police Integrity in the Developing World

Building a Culture of Lawfulness

Heath B. Grant
Department of Law, Police Science and Criminal Justice
John Jay College of Criminal Justice
New York, NY, USA

ISSN 2192-8533 ISSN 2192-8541 (electronic)
SpringerBriefs in Criminology
ISSN 2194-6213 ISSN 2194-6221 (electronic)
SpringerBriefs in Policing
ISBN 978-3-030-00412-5 ISBN 978-3-030-00413-2 (eBook)
https://doi.org/10.1007/978-3-030-00413-2

Library of Congress Control Number: 2018954934

© The Author(s) 2018
This work is subject to copyright. All rights are reserved by the Publisher, whether the whole or part of
the material is concerned, specifically the rights of translation, reprinting, reuse of illustrations, recitation,
broadcasting, reproduction on microfilms or in any other physical way, and transmission or information
storage and retrieval, electronic adaptation, computer software, or by similar or dissimilar methodology
now known or hereafter developed.
The use of general descriptive names, registered names, trademarks, service marks, etc. in this publication
does not imply, even in the absence of a specific statement, that such names are exempt from the relevant
protective laws and regulations and therefore free for general use.
The publisher, the authors, and the editors are safe to assume that the advice and information in this book
are believed to be true and accurate at the date of publication. Neither the publisher nor the authors or the
editors give a warranty, express or implied, with respect to the material contained herein or for any errors
or omissions that may have been made. The publisher remains neutral with regard to jurisdictional claims
in published maps and institutional affiliations.

This Springer imprint is published by the registered company Springer Nature Switzerland AG
The registered company address is: Gewerbestrasse 11, 6330 Cham, Switzerland

Contents

1 Antecedents and the Nature of Police Corruption and Impunity in Postcolonial and/or Developing Countries 1
Back to the Basics – The Bad Apple in the Bunch 4
References.. 5

2 Integrity Training: The Importance of a Moral Resoning and Rigorous Evaluations 7
Defining Police Integrity...................................... 7
Individual Level Integrity 7
Organizational Level Integrity 8
Scope of Integrity Training.................................... 8
Pedagogical Techniques in Integrity Training..................... 9
Content of Integrity Training 9
Moral Reasoning as an Integrity Promotion Tool.................. 10
References... 12

3 Change in Police Organizations – Towards a Top Down/Bottom Up Strategy 13
References... 15

4 Why Civilian Oversight is NOT the Answer – Addressing Use of Force and Other Human Rights Violations................ 17
References... 19

5 Rethinking Community Policing – Collective Efficacy First 21
References... 23

6 The Not So Exemplary Example – Bangladesh National Police...... 25
Politics and the Police in Bangladesh............................ 26
The Ever-Present History of Partition............................ 26
Varied Attempts at Police Reform............................... 29

Community Policing: Strengths, Flaws, Implementation
and the Importance of Local Context 31
   Key Lessons for Implementing Community Policing Models
   in the Developing World...................................... 31
The Need for a Moderate Level of Police Legitimacy 33
Collective Efficacy as a Starting Point 35
Summary and Recommendations Moving Forward 36
References... 36

**7   Tying It All Together – I'm Smarter than a Ninth
Grader – The Culture of Lawfulness Model and Its Origins
in the Schools**... 39
Taking It to the Police.. 40
Education in the Rule of Law for Police.......................... 41
Conclusion 44
References... 45

About the Author

Heath B. Grant Prior to returning to the full-time faculty of John Jay College of Criminal Justice in 2013, Dr. Grant was most recently the Director of Research of the Police Executive Research Forum, a leading Washington DC organization dedicated to advancing law enforcement and crime prevention internationally. Formerly, as CEO, of Success for Kids (SFK), he oversaw the planning, implementation, curriculum development, partnerships & strategic program alliances and evaluation of the organization's international programs and services. A 15 year program executive, his experience and innovative style has positioned SFK's unique approach to Social Emotional Learning as one of the most sought after program partnership opportunities throughout Africa, the Middle East, Europe, and the Americas. On behalf of the Asia Foundation, he also recently developed training curricula for the Bangladesh National Police on community policing. He subsequently conducted an assessment there related to the status of community policing in the country.

Chapter 1
Antecedents and the Nature of Police Corruption and Impunity in Postcolonial and/or Developing Countries

Academics always run the risk of a passionate need to categorize the world, and even its most complex problems, into the single perspective or theory that most inspired us in our earliest study and entry into the real world of scholarship. If we are not careful, this single perspective or theory can function as a dominant lens capable of blocking all else out but the facts or data that support or affirm the theory or perspective that we came in with in the first place (Rosling 2018).

This is why responsible educators of new students in research methods and any of the social sciences must first stress that "even null findings are significant" and must be reported. In other words, even when we have results that are opposite to our research hypotheses, or that are themselves insignificant, these too tell us something important about the real world that we are trying to study, and hopefully, improve in some way. This is particularly important for the "pracademic" that seeks to bridge the worlds of academia and practice to support meaningful policy and program change as has been the focus of the current author's entire career.

Before even beginning, it is important to address a glaring example of our desire to categorize the world simplistically: the very title of this work suggests that there is both a "developing world", and one that is "developed". Rosling (2018) argues that this over simplification is a significant reason for why so many of us get it wrong when we think about the state of contemporary affairs globally. "When people say 'developing' and 'developed' what they are probably thinking is poor countries and rich countries…..West/rest." (Rosling 2018, p. 24).

Contrary to our worldview, "poor developing countries" no longer exist as a distinct group, although this was true years ago (Ibid). Most people in the world live in middle income countries. Of course, a small number of countries exist on either extreme of poverty or wealth.

You may be starting to wonder why you picked up this work. You set out to read and understand the problem of police corruption internationally rather than discuss

---

© The Author(s) 2018
H. B. Grant, *Police Integrity in the Developing World*, SpringerBriefs in Criminology, https://doi.org/10.1007/978-3-030-00413-2_1

the defining characteristics of "developing countries". In fact, this understanding has everything to do with getting the complexities of policing across the world right as well. As we will see, social indicators are related to police corruption, but it is far more complex than that. Even in more impoverished countries, the causes of police corruption cannot simply be explained away as a result of poor salaries and/or a lack of economic development even though a great deal of police scholarship and theory identifies the importance of these variables.

There is a diversity of causes for police corruption; these necessarily include the individual, organizational, and social levels of analysis. As is true in other sectors of society, "police are not good or bad. Police are many things". Understanding the causes of police corruption, at least sufficiently to build practically meaningful solutions, must start from this recognition of complexity.

Having had the opportunity to work with and train police officers from many countries, including those labeled the most corrupt, this complexity has always been readily apparent to the author. What becomes clear is that so many individuals that choose this profession often do so with the aspiration to truly make a difference in the world. Where this vision veers off course is usually a case by case situation on both the organizational and country levels, rather than simple the individual level captured in our "go to" policing stereotype of the "rotten apple in a barrel".

While facilitating a discussion on the nature and causes of police corruption with a group of new recruits in the Mexican Federal Police, the author noticed the concern and agitation on the face of one of the participants. He was alarmed at his colleagues' willingness to reduce the causes of corruption in the Federal Police down to the pressures of peers and the inability to turn to anyone in the command for support when corruption was going on. To him, the extreme of "plata o plomo" suggested that the problem was far more complex than that.

"Plata o plomo" literally refers to the idea that an officer must take the money being offered as a bribe or the lead of bullets from a gun. In some countries stricken by (particularly drug related) crime, cartels can threaten to kill an officer or his or her family as a consequence of not taking a bribe. Once the bribe is taken, the officer is left in a situation of having to take more in the future given the information the trafficker now has on him or her. And so it goes on.

Transparency International (2014) has identified the police as one of the most corrupt institutions internationally. Thus it is not surprising that most international anticorruption training or technical assistance efforts focus on the level of police departments to drive change. It is thought that with better implemented ethical codes (IACP 2014), or holding police supervisors accountable for the integrity of their subordinate officers (Klaver 2013), internal pressures for police deviance will subside. Of course, such strategies are best paired with prevention approaches that have been successful in the United States and elsewhere, such as implementing more rigorous forms of recruitment and selection. Extensive psychological tests and background investigations will screen out those that are most likely to engage in corruption and other forms of police deviance.

Newburn and Webb (1999) argue that strategies for the prevention and control of police corruption fall into four distinct categories. Each of these reflects a different understanding of the causes of police corruption:

- Human resource management;
- Anti-corruption policies;
- Internal controls; and,
- External environment and external controls

Subsequent chapters will argue for the importance of each of these areas in combating corruption, but also that it is the fourth, most often ignored category where most innovation needs to occur in order for sustainable, long-term change to take place.

According to Sherman (1978), the pressures from a corrupt political environment can provide the external pressure necessary to make a law enforcement agency corrupt. This is most apparent where government officials are able to use the police for their own personal and political purposes and gain, and especially where the rule of law is weakened by a lack of separation between powers. If the judicial branch does not have the will or ability to hold the police accountable, police corruption will be both pervasive and inevitable.

This cause of corruption is certainly a factor in many of the countries we are calling "developing" for the purposes of this book. But most police scholars and practitioners often do not recognize that the external environment facilitating police corruption invariable extends to the culture itself. And while the culture we are referring to includes the organizational culture of the police organization, it also extends to the social environment in which the police are embedded.

Williams (2002) argues that the cultural traditions of countries are a core factor of police corruption. The culture of a society places external pressure on the police officers to become corrupt. In such cultures, citizens may view police corruption as a necessary inconvenience that is just a part of doing business. Here, both the police and the citizens share negative attitudes towards the law and rule of law. Of course, accepting a cultural role in police corruption reflects the obvious: "it takes two to tango". Both an officer and a citizen are necessary ingredients of most forms of corruption (Klockars et al. 2003; Punch 2000).

Also complicating the issue is the fact that social indicators have been found relevant to the incidence of police corruption, such as life expectancy, education, religion, involvement of women in society, urbanization, and economic development (Diemont 2013; Garcia and Rodriguez 2016). Building off the author's earlier work in this series (Grant 2014), the author will help the reader to better understand the significance of such social and cultural factors in the prevention and control of police corruption, within a comprehensive framework that includes the individual level and organizational change approaches most commonly understood and pushed in the contemporary police and rule of law development practitioner industry. Others have also argued for the importance of taking society into account in designing reforms (Dutta 2011). More traditional approaches are in fact necessary in overall success, just not sufficient without including culture in the equation.

Back to the Basics – The Bad Apple in the Bunch

Newburn and Webb (1999) holds that most police organizations around the world have some common causal factors that contribute to police corruption due to the nature of the work itself. Of course, some of these causal factors will vary according to the internal and external pressures on police, but there are certain risk factors that must be considered by all agencies.

Although often an overly simplistic explanation as described above, many police corruption experts point to the discretionary nature of police work as a central issue. Police officers inherently have the ability to ignore or enforce the law while under minimal supervision in the community (Lauths et al. 2011). This invariably can open the door to corruption in unethical officers. Officers are thus vulnerable to taking bribes. Similarly, the ambiguity in the law itself, and the police mandate to interpret the law situationally can confound these challenges.. The Association of UK Chief Police Officer's Anti-Corruption Task Force (1999) famously captures the dilemma of policing this way:

> "Given the nature of police work, it is no shame to find corruption within the service: the shame is not doing anything about it"

The idea of the "slippery slope" of police corruption is commonly cited to represent the idea that individual police corruption for an officer often starts small and escalates over time (Sherman 1985). The metaphorical slope can begin with bribes and kickbacks before advancing to opportunistic theft, shakedowns, protection from illegal activities, and even to acts of serious violence. This analogy is significantly over-used in the field of policing, and has recently begun to be challenged. Recent research finds that often corrupt officers start their acts much higher up the chain of seriousness than once imagined. Either way, whether in the developing or developed world, the power, influence, and pressure of an officer's peers and supervisors continue to be recognized as playing central roles in the decision to engage in unethical behavior in its many possible forms (Caldero and Crank 2011).

When developing any strategic plan to combat police corruption, the police culture must be a key consideration even as we begin to think outside of the box and include an analysis of the external pressures in the larger culture as well. Successful and sustainable efforts should identify interaction points between the police and outside culture that increase the likelihood of corruption. At the risk of pointing out the obvious, the "police culture more or less reflects the values of the society that the police organization functions in" (Hobbs 1998).

The "blue wall of science" behind which police operate in secrecy and unshakeable loyalty to one another has been attributed to a culture that is defined by the danger of the profession and the constant risk of being exposed to public scrutiny (Skolnick et al. 2005). The expectations of citizens for police corruption then find a suitable opportunity structure in which to offer bribes or request unlawful protection as part of the business costs of interacting with the police in society.

Corruption in the developing world is often classified as predatory policing, which is "where police activities are mainly (not to say exclusively) devoted to the personal enrichment and self-preservation of individual officers rather than police protection of the public (Gerber and Medelson 2008, p. 2); however, predatory policing can also be found in the developed world too, of course. Yet since the early twentieth century, this type of police corruption, once widespread in the United States' "political era", has significantly declined (Kelling and Moore 1988; Caldero and Crank 2011). Arguably, other forms of corruption, such as noble cause corruption have become more prevalent in the United States and other developed countries.

Some scholars have argued that any police culture is directly influenced by the societal norms of the culture that it is embedded in (Punch 2000; Waddington 1999), painting a picture that may seem overwhelming to most police reformers on the international stage. Despite the complexity of the problem, police reformers in the developing world regularly cite improvements to police salaries and resources as an easy place to begin the processes of reform. Once again, while this may be a necessary factor to consider in bringing police reform to the developing world, it is not sufficient without developing a comprehensive systems approach that also includes approaches for the police and external cultures.

References

Anti-Corruption Task Force. (1999). Association of chiefs of police presentation at the European Council Conference on Police Corruption, Strasbourg, France, November 1999.

Caldero, M., & Crank, J. (2011). *Police ethics: The corruption of noble cause.* Burlington: Elseveir.

Diemont, E. (2013). The Natrure of Corruption: An Intedisciplinary Perspective. Economic Conversations.

Dutta, S. (2011). *The Global Innovation Index 2011: accelerating growth and development.* Insead.

Garcia, & Rodriguez. (2016). Social determinants of police corruption: toward public policies for the prevention of police corruption. *Policy Studies, 37*(3), 216–235.

Gerber, T. P., & Mendelson, S. E. (2008). Public experiences of police violence and corruption in contemporary Russia: A case of predatory policing? *Law & Society Review, 42*(1), 1–44.

Grant, H. (2014). *Social Crime Prevention in the Developing World: Exploring the Role of Police in Crime Prevention.* New York: Springer.

Hobbs, D. (1998). Going down the glocal: The local context of organised crime. *The Howard Journal of Criminal Justice, 37*(4), 407–422.

International Association of Chiefs of Police. (2014). *Model policy on standards of conduct.* Retrieved from http://www.theiacp.org/Model-Policy-on-Standards-of-Conduct

Kelling, G. L., & Moore, M. H. (1988). *The evolving strategy of policing.* Washington, DC: US Department of Justice, Office of Justice Programs, National Institute of Justice.

Klaver, J. J. (2013). Law enforcement ethics and misconduct. In B. D. Fitch (Ed.), *Law enforcement ethics: Classic and contemporary issues* (1st ed., pp. 3–28). Thousand Oaks: Sage Lauchs.

Klockars, C. B., Ivkovic, S. K., & Haberfeld, M. R. (2003). *The contours of police integrity.* Thousand Oaks: Sage Publications.

Lauchs, M., Keast, R., & Yousefpour, N. (2011). Corrupt police networks: Uncovering hidden relationship patterns, functions and roles. *Policing and Society, 21*(1), 110–127.

Newburn, T., & Webb, B. (1999). *Understanding and preventing police corruption: Lessons from the literature.*

Punch, M. (2000). Police corruption and its prevention. *European Journal on Criminal Policy and Research, 8*(3), 301–324.

Rosling, H. (2018). *Factfulness: Ten reasons We're wrong about the world – And why things are better than I think*. New York: Flatiron Books.

Sherman, L. W. (1978). Controlling police corruption: The effects of reform policies, *Summary Report*.

Sherman, L. W. (1985). Becoming bent: Moral careers of corrupt policemen.

Skolnick, J. H., Feeley, M., & McCoy, C. (2005). *Criminal justice: Introductory cases and materials*. New York: Foundation Press.

Transparency International. (2014). Global Corruption Barometer 2013. Retrieved from http://www.transparency.org/gcb2013/in_detail

Waddington, P. (1999, March 1). Police (canteen) sub-culture. An appreciation. *The British Journal of Criminology, 39*(2), 287–309. https://doi.org/10.1093/bjc/39.2.287.

Williams, H. (2002, December). Core factors of police corruption across the world. *Forum on Crime and Society, 2*(1), 85–99.

Chapter 2
Integrity Training: The Importance of a Moral Resoning and Rigorous Evaluations

Another regular "go to" in the anti-corruption tool box of rule of law development professionals is to implement some form of police integrity training.

Defining Police Integrity

The idea that integrity is essential to the effectiveness of police organizations has long been recognized by both the academic and practitioner communities internationally. However, there still remains a significant divide as to exactly how to define integrity, and whether or not the emphasis should be placed on individuals or organizations as a whole. As a result, there is also a split between those that think integrity is something that can be trained, or whether it can only be addressed through some combination of organizational incentives and consequences.

Individual Level Integrity

Most researchers defining police integrity on the individual level focus on a "fidelity, in speech and action" to the goals and values of the *profession* (Scharf 2006; Sykes 1993; Crank 1998). This emphasis on adherence to the values of the police profession requires further examination given the at times conflicting view of this internationally and the continuum of police practice from militaristic models to democratic policing principles.

Western policing scholarship tends to classify the goals of the police function into three distinct categories: order maintenance, enforcement of the law, and service to the community (e.g. Wilson 1975). The degree to which each of these functions is emphasized will vary according to the priorities of police leadership within

© The Author(s) 2018
H. B. Grant, *Police Integrity in the Developing World*, SpringerBriefs in Criminology, https://doi.org/10.1007/978-3-030-00413-2_2

a particular organization. In discussing the overarching values of the profession, democratic policing models stress the police role as representatives and adherents to the rule of law. Professional policing thus requires individual integrity as measured by the degree to which police functions are carried out with human dignity, tolerance, and respect regardless of the race, class, position, or any other special circumstance of people with whom the police interact (Scharf 2006).

Organizational Level Integrity

Many researchers believe that an agency's culture of integrity is more important in shaping the ethics of police officers than hiring the right people (Klockars et al. 2004). Although training can impact an officer's awareness of the rules and policies of an organization, it cannot change his or her ethics. There is no consensus on a definition for organizational integrity, but a synthesis of scholarship in the area focuses upon things such as the screening, early warning systems, training, and mechanisms for dealing with ethical violations. Adherents to the organizational focus for integrity have created checklists and surveys to rank the level of organizational integrity of police organizations.

Given the nature of police work, and the fact that there is often very little direct supervision of officers while they are working with the public, there is increasing recognition that consequences or sanctions will never be enough. Integrity cannot simply be based upon the degree to which officers know the rules and regulations and observe them simply because of variations in incentives and consequences (Vicchio 1997). There will always be too many opportunities and situations in which officers are beyond the reach of management to rest on this alone.

Although organizations cannot expect to create a cadre of highly ethical officers simply with training practices, comprehensive approaches to integrity management that combine best training practices with organizational reforms and incentives can make a difference in time on the overall culture of an organization, as we will discuss in the next chapter. Any integrity training needs to reflect this balance between individual and organizational integrity. The coordination needed to make it happen is almost never achieved in police training.

Scope of Integrity Training

As noted, stated concern for integrity training is not anything new within the United States or abroad. Integrity training is found in some form in most departments; however, 70% of agencies in a national study within the United States offered recruits less than 10 h of integrity training (Center for Society, Law, and Justice 2006). Even when such training is offered, it tended to focus more upon ethics appreciation than preparing officers for dealing with the real life problems they will be facing in the profession. Adequate ongoing emphasis on integrity practices by field training officers (FTOs) remains the exception rather than the rule. Additionally, many departments fail to continue with integrity training classes for mid-level managers and above, and even when implemented, they are often unfocused and offered on an optional basis only.

Pedagogical Techniques in Integrity Training

Gilmartin and Harris (1998) offer the following range of methodologies currently in use for integrity education:

- Power Point presentations
- Indoctrination
- Open discussion
- Socratic discussion
- Adult learning

Although each of these pedagogical techniques is used in integrity training.; internationally, the dominant method appears to be lecture oriented. Professional evaluations of the impact of integrity training remain scarce and inadequate, but the emerging consensus is that it must *emphasize the reasoning and critical thinking skills necessary to equip officers to solve the problems that they will encounter in the field* and be perceived as relevant and credible (Vicchio 1997). Adult learning approaches are also necessary to adapt training to the various learning styles of participants (visual, kinesthetic, and auditory), and ensure that the real life applications are readily apparent to the learners.

Content of Integrity Training

There has only been one comprehensive comparative review of police integrity training. This study by the Center for Society, Law, and Justice (2006) found the following topics are currently common in police integrity education throughout the United States:

- Philosophy of ethics – Mill, Kant, values, social contract theory (Rousseau), professional standards and case law, golden rule
- Context for ethical decisions – moral reasoning, slippery slope of corruption, loyalty vs., duty, techniques of neutralization (ways offers rationalize corruption), integrity dilemmas, and models for decision-making
- Specific integrity issues and behaviors
- Consequences of unethical behavior – lose promotions, divorce, firing (these tend to focus only on the individual level of consequences)

Moral Reasoning as an Integrity Promotion Tool

Although covered in some integrity training programs as part of the context for ethical decision making, few offer moral reasoning the central focus and pedagogical techniques necessary for it to be truly effective. Very little evaluation research has looked at the effectiveness of moral reasoning strategies neither; however, this is not surprising given the lack of integrity evaluations found in the policing literature overall.

As moral reasoning has been shown to lead to improvements in ethical decision-making (Kohlberg 1984), it should be looked at more closely as a means to enhance the effectiveness of police officer integrity training. Kohlberg's (1984) theory of moral reasoning suggested that individuals advance in levels of moral reasoning by encountering (and ultimately resolving) moral dilemmas. Improvements in ethical decision making can be found on the higher reasoning levels where decisions become driven by a desire to do the right thing, rather than a fear of punishment or other more selfish inclinations. Knowing how to navigate moral dilemmas leads to ethical behavior if it is not disturbed by external pressures or forces within the organizational culture.

Rest (1986) offers a four component model of moral decision-making that includes the moral reasoning concept. Similar to Kohlberg, Rest concluded that a moral dilemma triggers the development of moral reasoning or mental processes that produce a motivation and character to make difficult decisions, and ultimately act morally. Importantly, integrity and ethics training using this approach outside of the policing context have been shown to lead to improvements in moral sensitivity (Ritter 2006) and moral motivation and values (Wu 2003).

In any organizational culture, a socialization process occurs in which the individuals learn to appreciate the values, skills, and behavior necessary for taking on a role within it (Bennett 1984). As we have discussed, the organizational or police culture has developed a significant lore in the research and practice literature. It is often argued that a weakening of ethical principles occurs as recruits move out of the academy and into the guidance and direction of a field training officer that teaches them "how policing is really done" (Engelson 1999; Van Maanen 1978). Crank (2004) refers to this as becoming familiar with both the job context and the organizational culture as separate from what has taken place during the time in the academy. The essential consideration of requisite cultural change in policing will be examined in the next chapter.

Miller and Braswell (1992) argue that recruits can maintain their personal values and moral reasoning abilities, but pretend to have internalized the dominant values of the police culture when around their peers. The implication is that a grooming by training officers result in cadets altering their values to be more close to those of their training officers. Contrary to the more negative portrayal of the more problematic aspects of police culture, the little research that has been done on moral reasoning in policing has suggested that recruits maintain stable scores in moral reasoning throughout and following the one year police training period (Mumford et al. 2008); the data did not support the idea of a weakening of these skills over time.

There is also evidence to suggest that some moral reasoning focused training programs can lead to significant improvements in the moral reasoning skills of police recruits. This was the case even though several studies have suggested that many recruits already come to the academy with high scores on moral reasoning with little room for improvement (so difficult to show change pre and post training) (Mumford et al. 2008).

An outgrowth of the moral reasoning perspective is the "sense making approach" to ethics training. This type of training" stresses the importance of the strategies that people apply to make sense of ethical problems" (Mumford et al. 2008) such as the moral dilemmas discussed above. Although not tested with police participants, the sense making pedagogy has been shown to lead to improvements in the ethical decision making of pharmacology and life sciences scholars (Ibid). Evaluations of this method need to be conducted with police participants. In addition, the sustainability of sense making programs over time on ethical decision making and reasoning also needs to be looked at more closely.

The field practices training method might offer the most meaningful application of both the moral reasoning/sense making approaches and the need for recruits to be able to reconcile the complexity of dynamics in the field with the rigorous codes of conduct and guidelines of most law enforcement agencies. Such training revolves around field specific guidelines and codes of conduct as the core of the training (Gawthop and Uhlemann 1992). The training offers vague or undefined situations that allow them to use a variety of mental models to make cognitive sense of the situation. Participants learn a framework to gather information and apply agency standards to determine the best course of action. Thus, moral reasoning skills can be enhanced while also gaining concrete knowledge of the agency's own code of conduct. In addition to discussions related to the decision points in the presented situations, there is usually some form of role play and/or simulation to ensure the maximum meaning and transfer of learning for the participant. Evaluations offer positive conclusions about the effectiveness of sense making training to enhance both ethical decision-making and the application offered reasoning strategies.

To conclude, we have argued that education in ethics can in fact improve the level of moral reasoning and ability of trainees to successfully navigate complex ethical issues (Prentzler 2009; Grant 2006). The complexity of policing, and the known external pressures of its unique organizational culture mean that significant attention must also be paid to transformational efforts within the organization and the community in which it is embedded in order for sustainable and meaningful change to occur; this may be particularly (though not uniquely) true in developing countries. This will be the focus of our next chapter.

Finally, although the best results can be evidenced in sense making approaches that offer the most realistic portrayal of the realities of policing, some studies suggest that an overemphasis on the dangerousness of the job can lead to an erosion of cadets' pre-academy level of integrity; it has been suggested that` this may be because danger can be used as the justification for the unethical and illegal acts (Ford and Lawry 1986).

References

Bennett, R. R. (1984). Becoming blue: A longitudinal study of police recruit occupational socialization. *Journal of Police Science and Administration, 12*(1), 47–58.

Center for Society, Law, and Justice (2006). *Managing Law Enforcement Integrity: A Summary of Findings for Law Enforcement Leaders.* Washington, DC: Bureau of Justice Assistance.

Crank, J. (1998). *Understanding police culture.* Cincinnati: Anderson Publishing.

Crank, J. P. (2004). *Understanding police culture* (2nd ed.). Cincinnati, OH:Anderson.

Engelson, W. (1999). The organizational values of law enforcement agencies: The impact of field training officers in the socialization of police recruits to law enforcement organizations. *Journal of Police and Criminal Psychology, 14*(2), 11–19.

Ford, M. R., & Lowery, C. R. (1986). Gender differences in moral reasoning: A comparison of the use of justice and care orientations. *Journal of Cognitive style and Social Psychology, 50,* 777–783 d, 2003.

Gilmartin, K. M., & Harris, J. J. (1998). The continuum of compromise. *Police Chief, 65,* 25–28 Center for Society, Law, and Justice (2006).

Grant, H. (2006). *Building a Culture of Lawfulness.* New York: LFB Scholarly.

Klockars, C. B., Kutnjak Ivkovi, S., & Haberfeld, M. R. (2004). The contours of police integrity. In C. B. Klockars, S. Kutnjak Ivkovi, & M. R. Haberfeld (Eds.), *The contours of police integrity.* Thousand Oaks: Sage.

Kohlberg, L. (1984). *The psychology of moral development: Moral stages and the life cycle* (Vol. 2). San Francisco: Harper & Row.

Miller, L. S., & Braswell, M. C. (1992). Police perceptions of ethical decision-making: The ideal vs. the real. *American Journal of Police, 11,* 27.

Mumford, M. D., Connelly, S., Brown, R. P., Murphy, S. T., Hill, J. H., Antes, A. L., et al. (2008). A sensemaking approach to ethics training for scientists: Preliminary evidence of training effectiveness. *Ethics & Behavior, 18*(4), 315–339.

Prenzler, T. (2009). *Police corruption: Preventing misconduct and maintaining integrity.* Boca Raton: CRC Press.

Rest, J. R. (1986). *Moral development: Advances in research and theory.* New York: Prager.

Ritter, B. A. (2006). Can business ethics be trained? A study of the ethical decision-making process in business students. *Journal of Business Ethics, 68*(2), 153–164.

Scharf, P. (2006). Managing law enforcement integrity: The state of the art (A summary of Gawthrop, J. C., & Uhlemann, M. R. (1992)). Effects of the problem-solving approach in ethics training. *Professional Psychology: Research and Practice, 23*(1). 38.

Sykes, G. W. (1993). *Why police ethics?* Law Enforcement Ethics Center, Southwestern Law Enforcement Institute.

Van Maanen, J. (1978). People processing: Strategies of organizational socialization. *Organizational Dynamics, 7*(1), 19–36.

Vicchio, S. J. (1997). Ethics and police integrity. *FBI L. Enforcement Bull., 66,* 8.

Wilson, J. Q. (1975). *Varieties of police behavior: The management of law and order in eight communities.* Cambridge, MA: Harvard University.

Wu, C. (2003). A study of the correlations among ethical decision-making of employees, corporate business ethics and organizational performances: Comparing Taiwanese outstanding SMEs, general SMEs and large enterprises. *NTU Management Review, 11*(1), 232–260.

Chapter 3
Change in Police Organizations – Towards a Top Down/Bottom Up Strategy

The police are the most public face of the state (Marenim 1996; Grant et al. 2006). The treatment that people receive from the police is often a reflection of the fairness of government, and particularly the criminal justice system, Years of research on legitimacy has demonstrated that the more that citizens have faith in the police, the more they are likely to comply with the rules and laws of society. Of course, in many developing countries, treatment by the police can also reflect the extent to which the government supports the rule of law itself. Without professional policing, the chances of building a culture supportive of the rule of law, or a culture of lawfulness, becomes unlikely or extremely difficult (Grant 2014).

Police reform has often been characterized as being" piece meal" in nature by many police scholars (Goldstein 1990). Most cite a resistance to change that favors the status quo amongst most front line officers and even the management ranks (Rippy 1990). This resistance to change leaves even police managers that accept the need for transformation limiting themselves to traditional strategies such as training and new policy (Shearing 1995). Once again, these approaches are necessary, but not sufficient to create an organizational change capable of promoting a policing that conforms to the law (Ibid).

It is essential to reiterate here that police organizations, like any other organization, are motivated by many factors to recognize the need for organizational change. In addition to changing business partners, institutions, relationships between countries, and available resources, the "dominant values and norms of society will play an essential, if not predominant role (Beckhard and Harris, 1987). This returns us to our discussion of recognizing the culture in which police organizations are embedded before believing that sustainable organizational transformation is practical. This is true in police organizations anywhere. The challenges in developing countries with extreme levels of poverty, and a greater tolerance of crime and corruption are perhaps exaggerated.

A leading voice in accounting for the necessary components required for successful police cultural and organizational change is Janet Chan (1996). Important in Chan's work is the explicit recognition that not <u>all</u> police culture is oppositional, as

© The Author(s) 2018
H. B. Grant, *Police Integrity in the Developing World*, SpringerBriefs in
Criminology, https://doi.org/10.1007/978-3-030-00413-2_3

we also suggested in the previous chapter. In fact, she argues that not all police even within the same organization share the same culture: within one police organization there are different understandings and different commitments to the transformation process. For example, police managers and supervisors (top down) assume one way of looking at how things should be done that may or may not be shared with front line officers.

As such, Chan argues that there are 4 distinct levels of cultural knowledge within a police organization to consider when planning comprehensive change efforts:

1. Dictionary knowledge for the categories police have about those that they interact with in the course of their everyday interactions on the job (e.g. citizens on the street);
2. Dictionary knowledge that police have about the processes that can and should be followed to carry out their work;
3. Recipe knowledge – a menu of acceptable and unacceptable practices for handling situations and dilemmas as part of their work;
4. Axiomatic knowledge – basic understandings about the reason and vision for policing in society.

As the highest level of cultural knowledge, changes in the axiomatic knowledge of an organization can lead to significant changes on all other levels of police practice. However, it is of course not that easy. Chan stresses that deep and lasting change in the behaviors and habits of even front line officers requires balancing needed changes in the power structures and the ways line officers interact with the police manager and administrative commands. Structural and culture change need to occur concurrently, continuously reinforcing each other to achieve enduring change. In the immediate term, frontline officers (bottom up) will respond to the commands of their managers, but this will be superficial unless paired with top down structural changes as well. This would reflect lower levels of moral reasoning on the part of officers that cannot be counted on to withstand pressures outside of the immediate view of the span of control of their supervisor.

Other top police scholars have recognized the complexity of police cultural knowledge and its impact on behavior – and thus reject the "bad apple" theory of police corruption discussed in the first chapter. Klockars et al.'s (2004) multi—year comparative analysis of corruption articulates three distinct dimensions that are essential for understanding police integrity and culture within even complex developing world organizations.

The first dimension of organizational rule making refers to the creation and communication of organizational rules. Comparable to Chan's dictionary knowledge level, this dimension includes both formal and informal rules that communicate the expectation and rules of integrity, and the reasons for them.

The second dimension covers a range of activities that ensure the organization's accountability for police integrity. Integrity violations can be detected and enforced through proactive and reactive agency internal investigations, audits, and civilian complaint processes amongst others. In sum, this dimension supports the discipline of officers according to standards of integrity and is comparable to Chan's first dictionary knowledge level.

The third and final dimension offered by Klockars et al. (2004) covers the police organization's obligation to overcome the informal occupational culture of policing against reporting the misconduct of fellow police officers. Importantly, Klockars et al. (2004) have advanced the field by developing and implementing an assessment instrument capable of measuring the level of intolerance for misconduct in a police organization. Using carefully crafted scenarios of misconduct situations, the survey allows researchers and/or development practitioners to understand where there is a lack of knowledge about existing agency rules and standards (dictionary level), or worse, an apparent disregard for them entirely.

The picture painted for reformers is hopeful (even if very challenging) seeking to work with police organizations in developing countries plagued with problems of corruption and/or a general disregard for democratic policing and the rule of law. First, police culture is not inherently corrupt anywhere. A thorough assessment can point to where the problems are greatest. Then, a comprehensive plan that includes formal and informal learning needs to be embedded in the context of everyday police practice (Manuti et al. 2015). True experts in the field stress that organized programs alone will not be enough to reach truly transformational organizational change.

Recruit and in service training programs can offer needed dictionary level knowledge highlighting any changes in organizational standards and practices. Ideally, interactive sessions can help to build moral reasoning skills to better equip officers to negotiate challenging real world dilemmas. **An example of such a training program will be highlighted in Chapter Seven.**

Top down efforts can include technical assistance to police managers and executives in how to refine identified gaps in officer knowledge and practice through policy changes that offer consistent chances to role model professional behavior. Top down changes should also include modifications to the organization's performance incentive structure to further recognize practices that exemplify principles of democratic policing.

References

Beckhard, R., & Harris, R. T. (1987). Organizational transitions: Managing complex change

Chan, J. (1996). Changing police culture. *The British Journal of Criminology, 36*(1), 109–134.

Goldstein, H. (1990). *Problem-Oriented Policing.* New York: McGraw Hill, Inc.

Grant, H (2014). *Social Crime Prevention in the Developing World: Exploring the role of police in crime prevention.* New York: Springer.

Grant, H., Grabias, J., & Godson, R. (2006). The role of police in promoting the rule of law. In *Democratic policing in transitional and developing countries.* Routledge.

Klockars, C. B., Kutnjak Ivkovic, S., & Haberfeld, M. R. (2004). The contours of police integrity. In C. B. Klockars, S. Kutnjak Ivkovi, & M. R. Haberfeld (Eds.), *The contours of police integrity.* Thousand Oaks: Sage.

Manuti, A., Pastore, S., Scardigno, A. F., Giancaspro, M. L., & Morciano, D. (2015). Formal and informal learning in the workplace: a research review. *International journal of training and development, 19*(1), 1–17.

Marenin, O. (Ed.). (1996). *Policing change, changing police: international perspectives* (Vol. 14). Taylor & Francis.

Rippy, K. M. (1990). Effective followership. Police Chief, 57(9), 22–24.

Shearing, C. (1995). Transforming the culture of policing: Thoughts from South Africa. *Australian & New Zealand Journal of Criminology, 28*(1_suppl), 54–61.

Chapter 4
Why Civilian Oversight is NOT the Answer – Addressing Use of Force and Other Human Rights Violations

The title to this chapter might strike some as surprising and possibly unfair. When thinking about many police agencies in the developing world with notoriously high levels of reported corruption and human rights abuses (e.g. Brazil, Mexico and many others), why wouldn't the establishment of external citizen oversight be the right answer? Many would argue that this is the first thing that should take place.

In principle the idea of citizen oversight sounds like a good answer to the question of police abuse of power and corruption. If the police culture really promotes the unwavering loyalty that it is said to, how can police organizations ever be expected to hold themselves accountable? First, we have argued in previous chapters that police culture is not universally negative even within more corrupt and challenged organizations. Second, we have discussed the reality of several layers of police corruption within any one agency, requiring a comprehensive approach that takes into account multiple audiences and stakeholders.

Citizen involvement in policing does not have a stellar history, even within countries such as the United States. There, citizen involvement in the earliest days of policing in the United States often led to increased corruption, and decreased efficiency resulting from lower professional standards (Walker 2001). In fact, the evolution of professional policing as we know it today has involved a distancing of the police from citizen influence; of course, community policing models strive to reconnect citizens with police in terms of a joint ownership over problem solving the needs of the community. However, this does not include citizen oversight or influence in the internal running and operations of the department. We will return to the potential of community policing in developing countries in the next two chapters. For now, we will say that even community policing is not the obvious solution many might think it would be in the developing world either.

Leading citizen oversight scholar, Sam Walker, cites the inability to create a truly independent form of citizen oversight as one of "the fundamental dilemmas of accountability in a democratic society" (Walker 2001, p. 67). Of course this challenge is only aggravated further in many developing countries. Walker calls this issue a dilemma because of the challenge to have a body that is both truly independent

© The Author(s) 2018
H. B. Grant, *Police Integrity in the Developing World*, SpringerBriefs in Criminology, https://doi.org/10.1007/978-3-030-00413-2_4

of the police that remains responsive to the public through the normal avenues of democratic government.

Police are embedded in the local political system as an agency of local government. Similarly, any oversight agency will be a part of the same political system. If the political system itself is tolerant, or worse, supportive of corruption and other forms of police abuse, the independent agency will not have the power or resources to mandate or recommend policies or procedures that can hold the police organization accountable in a meaningful way.

As we have cited previously, this concern is only heightened when there is not a real separation between the executive and judicial branches, which is a very real situation in many developing countries. Mexico has struggled with this lack of an independent judiciary for decades, although reform is underway currently. In the end, if there is no will or capacity of judges to hold the police accountable (individually or as organizations), then any "independent" oversight agency is going to very likely be crippled in its ability to manifest true accountability. *How can independence be balanced with responsiveness in a way that can lead to the accountability that such agencies were created for in the first place?*

Some advocates have argued that making members of an independent citizen oversight agency elected would address these problems of a corrupt or inefficient political system. This fails to consider the importance of the cultural values of the larger society in which the police organization is embedded. If society is generally tolerant of police corruption, or sees it as a necessary part of interacting with the police, these elected members would likely reflect this.

Before we take the position that crime and corruption is too overwhelming to achieve any form of true police accountability, we need to remember that some police scholars and practitioners have argued that the essential features of democratic policing itself are responsiveness and accountability (Bayley 1997). Of course, by responsiveness Bayley is referring to the degree to which police respond to the needs of the public across the diverse sectors that it represents. To him, democratic policing can only be responsive if it also is "accountable to multiple alliances through multiple mechanisms".

Accountability in democratic policing will include the top down mechanisms that were discussed earlier such as training programs, early warning systems, and complaint review. A form of citizen oversight might also be effective as another check to make recommendations to the police executive about individual officer disciplinary sanctions and/or needed management reforms.

The point to be made here is that citizen oversight is not the panacea that many outside the police profession advocate for to ensure the "promotion and protection of the basic rights of the people and compliance with the law...(that are)... twin pillars of good policing in a liberal democratic society" (Sen 2010, p. 1).

Given the centrality of the police to newly forming democracies (Hinton and Newburn 2009), as the police are themselves a reflection of the fairness of government and the criminal justice system (Tyler and Wakslak 2004), it is worth providing here Sen's (2010) features of democratic policing; he argues democratic policing is both process and an outcome with the following features:.

"The key features of democratic police are:

1. It is accountable to the law and not a law unto itself, democratic policing requires that the police act within the boundaries of the law and within international standards. Those who break the laws face consequences through internal disciplinary systems and criminal law.
2. It is accountable to democratic structures and the community. This is necessary to ensure that police do not get identified with a single seat of power.
3. The police should be transparent in its activities. Most of the police activities should be open to scrutiny and subject to reports to regular outside bodies.
4. When there is transparency, community's cooperation is more assured and information more likely to be shared and this in turn is likely to help better crime control and order maintenance.
5. It must be a professional service governed by a code of ethics.
6. It should be representative of the community it serves. Police organizations that represent the community they serve are more likely to enjoy the trust of the community and particularly of the vulnerable and marginalized groups who need their protection most." (Sen 2010, p. 9)

Although civilian oversight can clearly play an important role in achieving democratic policing, it is not the only way to ensure transparency and democratic standards. Sen (2010) argues that it should be a part of a comprehensive approach to democratic policing. While this author of course agrees that it is an important component of needed police reform in most developing countries, civilian oversight should only be chosen as a strategy after a solid assessment of the degree to which the police organizational culture, and the larger culture it is embedded in, are themselves supportive of the rule of law.

References

Bayley, D. H. (1997, October). The contemporary practices of policing: A comparative view. In *Multinational Peacekeeping–A Workshop Series. A Role for Democratic Policing.*
Hinton, M., & Newburn, T. (2009). *Policing Developing Democracies.* New York: Routledge.
Sen, S. (2010). *Enforcing police accountability through civilian oversight.* New Delhi: SAGE Publications India.
Tyler, T. R., & Wakslak, C. J. (2004). Profiling and police legitimacy: Procedural justice, attributions of motive, and acceptance of police authority. *Criminology, 42*(2), 253–282.
Walker, S. (2001). *Police accountability: The role of citizen oversight.* Belmont: Wadsworth Thompson Learning.

Chapter 5
Rethinking Community Policing – Collective Efficacy First

For decades now, community policing has been the focus of many training and technical assistance efforts, both within the United States and abroad. The term "Community Era" (Wilson and Kelling 1978) has even been applied to the contemporary field of policing given the emphasis on this approach to police operations and crime prevention. Despite its broad international appeal and logical connection to the urban issues of much of the developing world, there exists a dizzying array of evaluation research studies that have produced very mixed results regarding its ability to impact crime, and even fear of crime.

Above all, the effectiveness of community policing strategies ultimately "depends on the good will of the public to be effective" (Alpert et al. 1998). In much of the developing world, particularly in Latin America, the extremely high levels of crime and impunity and the lack of trust in the police due to corruption have made the idea of community policing very appealing. Community policing is often seen as the most direct way to build a sense of police legitimacy in these communities for better or worse.

However, it is precisely because of the very low levels of police legitimacy and the overall dysfunction of the state and other sectors of society to address even basic needs in some of these communities that community policing might be entirely the wrong model to start with in developing countries.

The point of this chapter will not be to summarize the evidence-based literature surrounding community policing. Many other entire works have been dedicated to just that. Instead, the discussion will highlight ways in which the intellectual tradition surrounding social disorganization and collective efficacy offer the greatest potential for understanding how police collaboration with citizens in the developing world might be best achieved given its unique challenges and issues.

Social disorganization has long been linked to crime in criminology (Shaw and McKay 1942). Social disorganization is evident when the community structure is not able to maintain effective social controls or reflect the values of its residents (Shaw and McKay 1942). In other words, the community lacks the networks, norms,

© The Author(s) 2018
H. B. Grant, *Police Integrity in the Developing World*, SpringerBriefs in Criminology, https://doi.org/10.1007/978-3-030-00413-2_5

and trust that are required to stand against crime and corruption (Coleman 1990). These social ties have since been termed social capital in the research and practitioner communities (Ibid).

For decades community policing advocates have argued that it is the antidote to these often impoverished, high crime communities because the police and the community can work together to build networks, co-identify the causes of community problems, and mobilize the resources to implement effective crime reduction strategies. However, the challenges of crime in the developing world, particularly the very high crime urban communities of Latin America make these previously commonly understood assumptions impractical at best.

In communities overrun by crime in places like Ciudad Juarez, there may be tight networks already in place, but these networks may actively work against crime reductions and social control. In some of these communities, crime and criminals may be looked up to, while the police and state authorities are legitimately seen as corrupt and not worthy of collaboration (Grant 2014; Wilson 1996). Similarly, Pattillo-McCoy 1999) has argued that local networks (informal and formal) can also negatively assist organized crime, just as they can help to reduce drugs and gangs on the positive side. It should be stressed that these conclusions might be equally true of high crime communities in developed countries. The big difference is that in the developing world the criminal justice agencies also often lack a baseline level of legitimacy from which to start.

In recent years, the concept of "collective efficacy" has emerged as likely more practical and meaningful in considering community crime prevention approaches. Sampson et al. (1997) linked the trust and cohesion of residents to shared expectations of social control, including crime. This resolved the gaps in understanding that networks could be both positive and negative, and the finding that weak ties may be more characteristic of many communities in a prosocial way (Higgins and Hunt 2016). This re-tooling of the social disorganization and social capital concepts came to be known as collective efficacy. Portes and Sesenberenner (1993) explain it as "expectations for action within a collectivity" (1993:1323).

For the reasons discussed in this chapter, community-based crime prevention in the developing world should first consider two key elements before turning to community policing models: 1) a foundation of police legitimacy to begin to connect to existing community networks; and, 2) sufficient levels of collective efficacy to serve as a springboard for possible community policing efforts in the future.

As stated previously, community policing depends on the good will of the people (Alpert et al. 1998): collective efficacy should build this good will by first ensuring that existing networks can be mobilized for prosocial action, and that the police are viewed with a baseline of pre-existing legitimacy.

But where to begin in the most ravaged communities of the developing world when there is likely very little collective efficacy to work with and from? In even the most challenged communities there are usually places where residents naturally gather or connect. These can be parks, a bodega, a community center, etc. . Calling these "anchor points", Uchida argues that these should be the focus of early community assessment efforts, and the place from which collective efficacy can begin to be developed (Higgins et al. 2016).

References

Alpert, G., Dunham, R., & Piquero, A. (1998). On the study of neighborhoods and the police. *Community Policing: Contemporary Readings*, 309–326.

Grant, H. (2014). *Social crime prevention in the developing world: Exploring the role of police.* New York: Springer.

Higgins, B. R., & Hunt, J. (2016). Collective efficacy: Taking action to improve neighborhoods. *NIJ Journal, 277*, 18–21.

Pattillo-McCoy, M. (1999). *Black picket fences.* Chicago: University of Chicago Press.

Portes, A., & Sensenbrenner, J. (1993). Embeddedness and immigration: Notes on the social determinants of economic action. *American Journal of Sociology, 98*(6), 1320–1350.

Sampson, R. J., Raudenbush, S. W., & Earls, F. (1997). Neighborhoods and violent crime: A multilevel study of collective efficacy. *Science, 277*(5328), 918–924.

Shaw, C. R., & McKay, H. D. (1942). *Juvenile delinquency and urban areas.* Chicago: University of Chicago Press.

Wilson, W. W. (1996). *When work disappears: The world of the new urban poor.* New York: Alfred A Knopf.

Chapter 6
The Not So Exemplary Example – Bangladesh National Police

The case example of Bangladesh exemplifies many of the challenges that we have been speaking about thus far with respect to policing in the developing world. The Bangladesh National Police is a very large force that is very strapped for necessary resources to be able to effectively police – both within the large urban center of cities like Dhaka to the very remote villages characteristic of the countryside. Bangladesh is a country characterized by both extreme poverty and high levels of corruption on the part of its police and other government services.

In recent years, Bangladesh has also faced numerous religiously motivated murders of secular bloggers, activists, and members of the LGBT community (The Economist 2016). Unfortunately, these murders are coupled with an increase in other forms of violent extremist attacks that have contributed to an air of insecurity for many in the country. In 2007, the overall crime rate was 91.5 per 100,000 people, with property crimes being the most frequently reported (Kashem 2010). The country also faces other forms of ethnic and politically motivated violence from diverse populations.

Within many ongoing and lengthy police reforms in collaboration with the Police Reform Program of the UNDP, the Bangladesh National Police have implemented a well-intentioned community policing program that included a training program with the support and resources of the Asia Foundation and the USAID. Although the levels and type of violence certainly make any police reform challenging, it is likely that the very likely low levels of police legitimacy and collective efficacy are also contributing to its ineffectiveness despite uncharacteristically high support for the idea of community policing at all levels of the national police force (Grant 2014).

This chapter is adapted and abridged from H. Grant, S. O'Reilly, and S. Strobl (2019, forthcoming). "The Role of Legitimacy in Police Reform and Effectiveness: A Case Study on the Bangladesh National Police" in Das, and D. Petersen (eds). *Proceedings from the International Police Executive Symposium.*

© The Author(s) 2018
H. B. Grant, *Police Integrity in the Developing World*, SpringerBriefs in Criminology, https://doi.org/10.1007/978-3-030-00413-2_6

Politics and the Police in Bangladesh

Former Inspector General of the Police and Bangladeshi police reform has described the nexus between politics and policing as the "criminalization of politics". Regular street violence and protests (*called hartels*) are often instigated by the country's major political parties and utilize the "strong arm" of the police along with fear inducing national shutdowns of all transportation, shops, courts of law, schools, etc. for up to 5 days at a time. The police involvement in such government actions contributes to the already low levels of legitimacy resulting from the wide perception of corruption and human rights abuses from the perspective of citizens. With regard to corruption in particular, Bangladesh was ranked 139 out of 167 reviewed countries within Transparency International's (TI) Corruption Perceptions Index in 2015 (Transparency International 2015).

In focus groups with the author, citizens regularly stated that this is the reality that stands out rather than the training and use of officers trained in "community policing strategies"- even the holding of community police forums in the thanas did not shake this perception. For instance, according to TI's 2013 index, 39% of citizens surveyed reported having paid a bribe within the previous 12 months, and 72% of those that did said this was specifically during dealings with the police. According to the survey, the main reasons for paying the bribe were simply to obtain services (58%), to speed things up (33%), to express gratitude (7%) or ultimately to acquire services at a cheaper rate than normal (3%) (Transparency International 2013). Furthermore, the 2012 index shows that citizen perceptions of key sectors most affected by corruption are the police (78% of respondents), with labor migration and land administration coming in at a close second and third (77 and 75.8% respectively) (Transparency International 2012).

The Ever-Present History of Partition

Today's Bangladesh achieved post-colonial status when, as part of India, it gained independence from British colonial rule during the Indian Independence Movement in 1947. As part of this process of decolonization, the country was partitioned into what is present day India and Pakistan, divided between West Pakistan and East Pakistan, or present-day Bangladesh. East Pakistan was slated by the British decolonizers as the territory of the Muslim Bengali people, while Hindu Bengali people were to migrate to the Bengali state within India. Mass migrations and ethnic violence characterized Partition, making both countries a fraught space for people caught betwixt and between the new notions of identity (defined religiously) and territory. Civil employees were allowed to choose where they wanted to land, but, as Feldman (2003) describes, the displacement's effect on institutional development was to create "uncertainty about its personnel... at a time when massive upheaval and dislocation called for political coherence and the securing of social order"

The Ever-Present History of Partition

(p. 118). As such, policing was in a severe state of flux and police officers chose between two countries, shifting from one side of the dividing line to the other.

Further, the lack of resources to shore up the institution once the social order began to settle made investing in new institutions difficult. Many of the resources promised Dhaka from Calcutta never materialized, leaving East Pakistan wanting in terms of administrative technology and capacity (Feldman 2003). According to Feldman (2003) and Zafarullah (2007), with the limited resources available the government established an elite cadre of generalist administrators, the Civil Service of Pakistan (CSP), derived directly from the colonial administrators known as the Indian Civil Service (ICS). Zafarullah's (2007) analysis described the CSP in contemporary Bangladesh as primarily serving to maintain itself, acting with great autonomy from the masses and often from politicians as well. These empowered bureaucrats are drawn from the same social backgrounds and education and enter a system of vertical integration, which only promotes from within. Coupled with frequent regime changes, the civil bureaucracy acted as a kind of institutional glue in an otherwise unstable power landscape.

The state maintains strong control over police operations and the budget, and "politicization" of the police is considered a major problem (Kashem 2010 p. 26) as is the case in many non-Western, British post-colonial nations. The entire force operates on a budget of approximately 400,000 million dollars, and is part of the country's internal revenues system, along with other additional public goods, such as education and health care. Because policing plays a far second fiddle within the political arena, corrupt practices are basically perceived to be a necessary evil to make up for any resulting budgetary shortcomings that limit police salaries and institutional resources. Frequently, officers must pay "out-of-pocket" for basic equipment, such as fuel for vehicles, bicycle and rickshaw transportation to investigate crimes, or even office supplies such as snacks, stationary, pens, paper and printer toner. This is difficult to do when, for example, at the bottom of the pay scale police make as little as 5500 taka (approximately 70 USD) per month and, at the middle level, the going salary is 23,000 taka (approximately 300 USD), with little opportunity for promotion.

As a result, low-level corruption is present in the form of bribes or baksheesh of approximately $100 taka (a little over $1 USD), and most frequently collected by police who have significant contact with the public, such as traffic or street cops. This complements some of the more high-level politically-supported corruption practices, such as government contracts awarded by senior police for improving facilities, or providing special protection to politicians or other elites. On top of the bribes involved in day-to-day operations, most officers must pay a political bribe to a particular party to buy their way into the system upon entering the police. This bribe can be anywhere between 60,000–100,000 taka (870–1450 USD), but it secures them a government job in exchange for allegiance to a particular political party. Members of parliament and other senior ranking government officials in turn support this process, by purchasing a quota of spots from to, in effect, "guarantee the loyalty" of incoming law enforcement officials. Officers who are desperate for access to a stable income, especially in rural areas, have been known to sell dowry, family assets such as land or cattle, and/or even take out a loan from the village loan shark (International Crisis Group 2009) to obtain these spots.

Upon taking power, every incoming successive government since independence has made a practice of removing the majority of all top police and other government officials installed during the previous administration's time in office, and promoting new ones loyal to the current political party to take their place. For example, during the 2001–2006 Bangladesh National Party administration, almost 800 police officers were dismissed on political grounds, while 1000 were encouraged to retire and 65 senior officers were sacked. This approach not only disrupts the natural chain of command within police hierarchy, combined with other corrupt practices, it also reduces the functionality of basic police skills and their application in daily operations.

Notwithstanding the day-to-day corrupt practicalities for covering daily work and other police-related expenses, Gould et al. (2013) advances a larger systemic explanation for the different levels of corruption that exist across the police, and throughout Bangladesh, based on the need for political allegiances. According to his theory, at Partition, the government, and in particular police, were highly unpopular, as the despotism of the Raj was criticized widely, and the Indian independence movement was in full swing. In India and Pakistan, hope that the new government would reform colonial institutions, including the police, was quite high. Unfortunately, the form that Partition took, as a violent and catastrophic breaking of the very social fabric across the former colonized space, led to a weak political and social foundation. Groups struggled against each other in violent contests for local power and control, often targeted for inclusion or exclusion in new government agencies based on ethnic identity. Minorities in any space were seen in a suspicious light, and civil servants who relocated during the upheaval hoped to find jobs in their new space. As a result, loyalty doubts exited across the social spectrum and the uneven access to working in government, including jobs like policing, led to a flux in available services. Coupled with physical and economic insecurity, ordinary people turned to informal practice to secure what they needed and advance their everyday interests in accordance with a political culture supportive of such corruption. Subsequent anti-corruption, social and political movements ultimately were ineffective, and were unfortunately often used to fight vendettas against political enemies. Given that, since Partition, the country has moved through military rule and into post-civil war modes of one-party domination, the sense of trust and legitimacy in the police and other political agencies remains low and only intensifies the initial divides that existed between social groups, as well as now between government, police and the citizens they serve.

Even before the most recent period of questionable human rights practices by the Bangladeshi police, Rafiqul and Solaiman (2003) documented the routinized nature of police torture in Bangladeshi police custody. From 1972 until 2003, the researchers reported that there were 19,000 police custody deaths in Bangladesh, with only a handful of them ever tried as crimes, despite being contrary to the Constitution of Bangladesh's provisions for the right to life and personal liberty

(Article 32), equality before the law (Article 27), protection of law (Article 31), and safeguards against arrest and detention (Article 33).

Today, Bangladesh police and security forces continue to use excessive force in managing street protests, most recently killing 150 protesters, and injuring at least 2000 between February and October 2013 alone (Human Rights Watch 2013). As part of these operations, police and the paramilitary Rapid Action Battalian (RAB) often indiscriminately fire into crowds, and are known to brutally beat protesters (Ibid). Many of the protests that police have reacted to in the last couple years are part of a public outcry (both in favor of and against) decisions from the International Criminal Tribunal regarding war crimes, such as genocide, rape and crimes against humanity, committed during the 1971 Liberation War. These war trials are perceived by many to be directed toward punishment against opposition leaders, and do not have legitimacy from any type of international buy-in despite the name of the tribunal.

Varied Attempts at Police Reform

Since the 1971 split from then West Pakistan, Bangladesh has been host to more than half a dozen committees created to promote police reform and modernization of the system. Included within these is the Police Reform Programme (PRP), launched in 2005 by the Ministry of Home Affairs, with financial support of over ten million pounds from the UNDP and the British Department for International Development (DFID) during two phases: Phase I from 2005–2009, and Phase II from 2009–2014. PRP has been lauded as one of the biggest efforts of its kind with a focus on improving crime prevention, investigations, operations, prosecutions, human resource management, training and strategic capacity and oversight.

Significant results that have come out of the program, including the investigation of over 17,000 corruption cases by a recently created internal oversight unit, the first ever strategic planning process, a considerably more structured approach to community policing, and a proposed 2007 Police Ordinance meant to supplement the outdated 1861 Police Act. One of the biggest successes touted by PRP is the model police station, or *thana,* effort. As the lowest, albeit most publicly visible, operating space for the police, the *thana* is one of the institution's most important units for the police, and fostering one that can effectively respond to the demands of the public is crucial for success. The PRP's Model Thanas (MTs) have been set-up in various districts across the country to "showcase the best practices in policing by fostering an environment that facilitates prevention of crime, provides equitable access to justice and engages the police and public in a meaningful partnership to effectively address community concerns". The MTs are encouraged to use a pro-people, service-oriented form of policing, and have standard operating procedures that encourage reform at the most basic level of the police (See Police Reform Programme Phase II).

Notwithstanding the positive advances made by PRP, the system of implementation has not been without its complications. For instance, the difference between MTs and regular police stations is stark, and the impact this has on both available resources and delivery has been significant. Those officers and citizens in neighborhoods that don't benefit from the resource boost are often left questioning why the next *thana* over has received not only an increase in resources, but also in visibility, as a result of the change. As part of this, there are also concerns that the method for deciding in which districts MTs will be placed is opaque, and even politically motivated, and recent allegations of corruption have brought under question the entire process. Specifically, a March 2015 article in the Daily Mail claimed that the DFID funding for police *thana*s was actually being "used to help corrupt regimes stamp out political opposition" in multiple countries where it operates around the world. The article cites a study by the Independent Commission on Aid Impact, which warned that many of the *thana*s, which received enhanced equipment, training and financial support, were also the same locations that saw an increase in victimization (48%) and a tripling in the number of bribes paid to officers (Groves 2015).

Beyond issues surrounding the MTs; however, there are also questions regarding what the 2007 Police Ordinance never passed. This draft ordinance was created under PRP by a reform committee led by ex-IGP A.S.M. Shahjahan, and included a vision for an eleven-member National Police Commission, a Police Complaints Line, Police Tribunal and separation of police operations from political intervention (BD News 24 2008). However, after awaiting approval within the Ministry of Home Affairs for over 3 years, the Additional Secretary eventually gave a public statement "that the proposed ordinance is unrealistic and impractical" in nature, and could not be implemented. Based on this public statement, and closed door discussion held amongst a number of district commissioners at the time, it is believed that the ordinance was tabled for fear of creating too much political independence among the police (Daily Star 2010).

Besides the UNDP / DFID supported PRP, a number of other organizations have also provided technical assistance to the Bangladesh National Police, especially as it relates to community-based policing practices. These include the Japanese International Cooperation Agency (JICA), the Department of Justice's International Criminal Investigative Training and Assistance Program (ICITAP) and The Asia Foundation (TAF), the latter of which has been quietly promoting a grassroots approach to community policing in 20 locations communities since 2008. TAF's efforts received significant recognition and an increase in funding in early 2011, when USAID backed a three million dollar TAF-led Community-Based Policing (CBP) initiative in 518 communities across northwest Bangladesh. CBP was paired by the US Embassy as the citizen or community-led arm of the ICITAP's classroom-based approach taught at the police academy to all new incoming police officers. More about these efforts to promote community policing are discussed in the section below; however, it's important to note that these other programs receive only limited commitment from the Bangladesh National Police, being that they could not offer the significant equipment and financial incentives provided by PRP.

Community Policing: Strengths, Flaws, Implementation and the Importance of Local Context

In 2008, the PRP introduced a national strategy for community policing. The PRP provides a framework for the community policing approach; however, it was never officially approved by the Ministry of Home Affairs because its true application would require de-politicization of, and releasing control of field operations to, the police. That said, many officers still continue to reference the national strategy as a guide for community policing. In fact, senior leaders such as the current Inspector General of Police, Mr. Shahidul Hoque, who has been a strong supporter of community policing, have promoted the document as a benchmark for implementation among more junior ranks across the country.

The national strategy for community policing provides a clear definition of what it is, and how it aligns with international best practices through an organizational philosophy involving citizen-police partnerships and problem-solving. Still, the interpretation of this definition at the field level varies widely, often lending itself to extensive citizen involvement in police operations. In part, this has been done to fill a need created by limited internal staff and resources, but is also based on a history of mobilization of popular support from communities to push social movements and political agendas. In essence, what it involves is a "deputization" of citizens who lead patrols, capture criminals and basically serve as a force multiplier in police operations. This reflects a high level misinterpretation of the meaning of community policing which ordinarily is not a "force multiplier" meant to augment a lack of police resources.

In some cases, this has empowered citizens to go so far as to dictate how police should run operations, rather than giving them with overall support by gathering information, providing testimony, or just generally following the law. In fact, there have been numerous reports of citizens who were even given firearms by police to support their efforts in street patrols. This overt involvement in and control of police operations by citizens is often done by community leaders with strong political or social agendas, and has resulted in the persecution of minority groups or members of the opposing political party, in the name of rooting out terrorism. In some cases, citizens involved in the strategy have themselves asked for bribes from other citizens for services.

Key Lessons for Implementing Community Policing Models in the Developing World

This kind of misinterpretation of the community policing model is not uncommon, and has been seen when introduced in other developing countries as well, such as in South Africa and Guyana where community policing has become a highly racially and politically charged endeavor, or Honduras, where some neighborhood Security

Committees have transformed into self-defense groups in areas plagued by gangs and violence. In the case of Bangladesh, alternative interpretations have delegitimized community policing by making it about political party loyalty and eliminating any true representation of, or possibility to, address wider community needs.

Beyond the definition of community policing, the national strategy provides guiding principles for the implementation of Community Policing Forums (CPFs). Approximately 20,000 of these forums were created across the country, based on orders provided by police headquarters in 2008, to encourage spaces where citizens and police could partner on problem-solving key crime challenges in their community. However, representatives from civil society and the police report the forums were created under great time and political pressure, and many of the CPF members who were identified by the police to participate at that time were chosen based on their political leadership and alliances within the community; furthermore, these police-identified members often required the approval of the national political party, highlighting once more the problem of the politicization of the police.

Likewise, most of these forums have not been reactivated since their creation in 2008 and, as a result, the membership lists are outdated, with names of individuals who have either died or moved on. Furthermore, there is a lack of clarity regarding what types of crimes CPFs should address, with most covering a range from petty theft, to conflict over dowry, child marriage, gender-based violence, land disputes and even the threat of terrorism. In the case of gender-based violence, this frequently results in CPF members promoting their own interpretation of the law among community members, often by encouraging victims of domestic violence or sexual harassment not to press charges.

Additionally, while community policing has received substantial support among senior police, implementation is still uneven across the police. In part, this is because there are no structured incentives for promoting the community policing ethos. Community policing is not part of an internal evaluation process, institutional procedures, or daily protocols, and officers who apply it on the job are not rewarded for their efforts, but rather are perceived as working against the institutional culture of the police. This lack of internal organizational mechanisms contradicts the multitier identified as necessary to lead organizational cultural transformation efforts discussed in Chap. 3. Without these, the community policing model is limited to a training program alone in the long run. Perhaps most damaging, the "face" of its efforts remain the poorly trained, uneducated and under resourced constables that the public most often interacts with at the thana level.

This issue regarding the "face" of community policing is aggravated by the fact that the national strategy actually designates the creation of Community Policing Officers (CPOs) as a means for concentrating the responsibility of community policing efforts among a few select individuals at police stations.

While in theory this would appear to prioritize community policing, in practice many police stations don't have assigned CPOs, which provides an opportunity for sub-inspectors in charge of police stations to either deemphasize or eliminate community policing from daily operations. Furthermore, the regular rotation of police officers, often times as frequent as every 6 months, limits law enforcement's ability to develop a real connection or partnership with the communities where they work, which is a foundational part of the community policing approach. The result of this is that community policing is implemented on an ad hoc basis, usually because of the personal initiative of a given officer or his superiors at a specific police station, or because of targeted donor attention in a particular *thana,* instead of through national support and the provision of institutional incentives. Such a "specialization" of community policing was a common experience as such models evolved in the United States, the United Kingdom and elsewhere as well. *There should be no reason for technical assistance providers from the developed countries to assume that this would not be the case in the developing world as well.* The need to combine traditional training approaches with organizational change efforts MUST be articulated into the strategy from its earliest point of implementation.

These ongoing challenges raise the question of whether or not importing western models like community policing actually works. While there has been significant progress in creating a national mandate for community policing, the BNP has yet to develop a lasting organizational structure with a policy, budget and strategic planning process supportive of best practices in citizen-police relations. This limits the incentives for sustainable implementation of a community police model that, unless truly contextualized and tied to institutional procedures, has the power to move beyond strong national and community-level politics. In this sense, exporting Western models of policing without proper understanding or consideration for the socio-political context can lead to disastrous results, particularly in the challenging environments of post-colonial societies. The example of failures in the, even well intentioned, implementation of community policing in the Bangladesh National Police point to at least two important necessary conditions prior to choosing to providing community policing training and technical assistance in a post-colonial country: (i) a moderate level of police legitimacy and (ii) community-level collective efficacy as a starting point.

The Need for a Moderate Level of Police Legitimacy

Since its early British post-colonial origins, the BNP became alienated from the masses and their cultural practices. In other words, there has never been even a modicum of legitimacy for citizens. Legitimacy refers to the degree to which individuals believe an institution or authority is appropriate and proper. When an institution is perceived as a legitimate authority by the people, it reflects a belief that it is to be trusted, and its directives obeyed. As a result, legitimacy has a direct influence on individuals; rule violation (Tyler and Wakslak 2004). Without legitimacy, the average citizen (whether law abiding or not), will also not be willing to interact with the police in the meaningful way required for community policing strategies to be successful. According to a study by Kane, a lack of police legitimacy can be associated with more crimes by citizens. The research suggested that the first indicator of compromised police legitimacy, police misconduct, was linked to more violent crime in high and extremely disadvantaged neighborhoods, controlling for factors such as residential stability, youth population, and spatial and temporal effects. The rule of law represents justice: the more society and/or citizens move away from the rule of law, the more crime-prone they are. This means implementing community policing strategies in post-colonial contexts is even more dubious and challenging.

Community policing advocates might argue that this is looking at the theory of change in the wrong direction. Instead, community policing strategies should be implemented in such societies in order to build needed legitimacy for the police in the first place.

Although it is true that the successful police-community interactions of select community policing strategies can produce outcomes of legitimacy, the Bangladesh experience suggests that this is very unlikely in post-colonial contexts involving extreme political corruption, human rights abuses, and extensive legacies of citizen mistrust. In Bangladesh, citizens report that the types of officers they are more likely to engage with on a daily basis in the streets are not actually the few CPOs assigned to do community policing at the *thanas,* but rather the poorly trained constables that represent policing to the average citizen. These individuals make up the majority of the police force, and have little power to make decisions or engage with citizens on solving general crime and violence problems, and instead must wait for orders from more senior officials before taking any significant action. The constables' low capacity, and the BNP's use of them as the 'frontline' in the community, continues to limit institutional legitimacy. In these cases, community policing strategies may even exacerbate the problem of a lack of legitimacy if implementing authorities are not careful given the disconnect between community challenges and external political factors affecting the ability to form meaningful police-community partnerships needed for true proactive problem-oriented activities.

Future efforts to build police legitimacy of the Bangladesh National Police may require an increasing separation from the Ministry of Home Affairs and the close control it represents to the political party in power. However, this is likely not the best place to begin. Where a lack of legitimacy is a prolonged, entrenched reality (as in the case of the BNP), it may make good sense to first lay the seeds for community policing efforts within the community itself through development of a sense of collective responsibility for community safety, or collective efficacy as discussed in Chap. 5.

In Bangladesh, well-intentioned external development support such as those from USAID/TAF, UNDP and others ended up simply pushing the community policing model without contributing, or paying attention to the larger needed elements of police reform and professionalization that is necessary for citizen security to truly take root. In fact, this is the case of UNDP in particular, because it supports the wider Police Reform Programme, its officers were set-up directly within police headquarters in Dhaka. While this provided greater access to senior police officials and allowed the UNDP to introduce a number of important initiatives – such as the 2007 Police Act, and the national community policing strategy – it also impacted the neutrality of some UNDP staff, who were often overly sympathetic to police challenges of corruption, and reasons to not push a reform agenda too much.

Without a sophisticated analysis of the socio-political realities in post-colonial societies, implemented Western models of policing will ultimately "take the shape" of these structures beneath the surface in a way that is counter-productive to their original intent.

Collective Efficacy as a Starting Point

The legacy of post-colonial societies is a marked shift of the locus of control to the state. Police-citizen interactions are more transactionally based in a way that can easily give way to corruption. Superimposing community policing strategies and philosophy on top of this without first addressing the issues leading to a lack of legitimacy will not rectify the situation.

In recent years, the community-based crime prevention literature has identified the importance of collective efficacy, or a neighborhood's trust, cohesion, and shared expectations for control (Sampson et al. 1997) as being an important ingredient in crime reduction. Creating such shared expectations among citizens for engagement in social control may be a necessary first step to community policing strategies in post-colonial societies to successfully move beyond the entrenched realities of corruption and abuse. By strengthening collective efficacy amongst minority or disadvantaged groups, citizens are more equipped to ensure police adherence to the higher standards and meaning of community policing models.

Thus, re-purposing the locus of control or collective efficacy of villages and/or neighborhoods can help to ensure a police-community partnership that is capable of working through the difficult realities required to simultaneously restore police legitimacy and successful crime prevention in the long run. Community *panchayat*s, or local conflict resolution councils of five or more elders, is one example of a move in this direction in South Asia, specific the southern Indian state of Tamil Nadu. Hoping to counter the fear and mistrust of the police that stems from the collective experience of colonial rule, *panachayat*s continute to operate as local social control and order maintenance institutions. Some local policing efforts have worked with *panchayat*s in order to address long-standing community problems, including violence, that have thwarted the modern policing modus operandi or arrest and criminal prosecution; however tension remains between *panchayat* elders and the police in a general sense across the region, mostly because there is no specific program or mechanism to govern the cooperation between the two different socio-legal traditions, one based on the individual rights in the modern state, and the other based on community norms and values (Vincentnathan and Vincentnathan 2009). Nonetheless, the notion that leveraging grassroots and traditional forms of order maintenance toward solving crime problems could have great potential in Tamil Nadu.

Further afield, the *sungusungu* movement in Tanzania in the 1990s is more promising as a precedent. In this case, community members organized to respond to the routine crime of stock raiding, gaining legitimacy through traditional village elders and clans. They became such an effective form of social and criminal control they were eventually absorbed into the state as an arm of community policing. Though there is some criticism that their absorption represented a co-option of their locally grounded roots, Heald (2009) argues that ultimately they have transformed state power at the local level into one that is more responsive to local concerns. She writes:

> Communities have taken back power, developed their own policing capacity and, in so doing, effectively reinvented themselves…In the same way, perhaps they have reformed and reclaimed the state, with the administration demonstrating an increasing responsiveness to the priorities of local communities, and allowing them a greater degree of autonomy in the management of their own affairs (p. 78).

Summary and Recommendations Moving Forward

Prior to the implementation of community policing models, time would be best spent on increasing the collective efficacy of citizens in places where there has been a historic lack of control or meaningful cooperation with the police. This will help to ensure that community policing remains focused on partnership related to relevant and important crime considerations. Needs assessments prior to the implementation of community policing should identify existing resident groups and the socio-political context of their relationship to the police. The extent to which culturally and/or locally significant forms of legitimacy can be leveraged is a key factor in the success of any program, thereby not reinventing the wheel, but rolling with the wheel already in play and using the cultural capital and collective efficacy already in place to some degree. Meaningful collaboration between citizens and the police will not be possible where the governing powers are involved in the selection and direction of who and how police and citizens problem solve towards crime prevention. Where this is so, the citizens will simply become a "voluntary" arm of the existing state-centered power relationship and dynamics.

Police legitimacy is a necessary ingredient prior to implementing community policing models. Without this, community policing models are more likely to reinforce existing power or transactional politics that will counter any possible benefits of its implementation.

References

BD News 24. (2008, January 1). *Draft police ordinance waits home ministry clearance.* Retrieved on 26 Sep 2016 from: http://bdnews24.com/bangladesh/2008/01/11/draft-police-ordinance-waits-home-ministry-clearance

Daily Star Editorial. (2010, August 23). *Whither draft police ordinance, 2007?* Article Retrieved on Dec 26, 2016 from: http://www.thedailystar.net/news-detail-151810

References

Feldman, S. (2003). *Bengali state and nation-making: Partition and displacement revisited.* UNESCO.

Gould, W., Sherman, T. C., & Ansari, S. (2013). "The Flux of the Matter": Loyalty, corruption and the 'Everyday State' in Post-Partition Government Services in India and Pakistan. *Past & Present, 219*(1), 237–279.

Grant (2014). *Social Crime Prevenyion in the Developing World: Exploring the Role of Police in Crime Prevention.* New York: Springer.

Groves, J. (2015, March 5). *Foreign aid 'Being Used to Stamp Out Political Opposition': Report cities schemes being used to train security services to track mobile phones.* Article Retrieved 26 Dec 2016 from: http://www.dailymail.co.uk/news/article-2980247/Foreign-aid-used-stamp-political-opposition-Report-cites-schemes-used-train-security-services-track-mobile-phones.html

Heald, S. (2009). Reforming community, reclaiming the state: The development of Sungusungu in Northern Tanzania. In D. Wisler & I. D. Onwudiwe (Eds.), *Community policing: International perspectives and comparative perspectives* (pp. 57–80). Boca Raton: CRC Press.

Human Rights Watch. (2013). *Bangladesh security forces kill protesters.* Retrieved on 26 Dec 2016 from https://www.hrw.org/news/2013/08/01/bangladesh-security-forces-kill-protesters

International Crisis Group. (2009). *Bangladesh: Getting police reform on track.* Accessed 27 June 2016 at http://www.crisisgroup.org/~/media/Files/asia/south-asia/bangladesh/182%20Bangladesh%20Getting%20Police%20Reform%20on%20Track.pdf

Kashem, M. B. (2010). Bangladesh. In D. Chu (Ed.), *Crime and punishment around the world, Vol. 3. Asia/Pacific* (pp. 24–37). ABC-CLIO: Santa Barbara.

Rafiqul, M., & Solaiman, S. M. (2003). Torture under police reprimand in Bangladesh: A culture of impunity for gross violations of human rights. *Asia-Pacific Journal of Human Rights and the Law, 2*, 1–27.

Sampson, R. J., Raudenbush, S. W., & Earls, F. (1997). Neighborhoods and violent crime: A multilevel study of collective efficacy. *Science, 277*(5328), 918–924.

The Economist. (2016, May 20). *Despotic in Dhaka* (p. 34). The Economist.

Transparency International. (2012). *Corruption perceptions index.* Accessed 27 June 2016 at http://www.transparency.org/cpi2012/results

Transparency International. (2013). *Corruption perceptions index.* Accessed 27 June 2016 at https://www.transparency.org/cpi2013/results

Transparency International. (2015). *Corruption perceptions index.* Accessed 27 June 2016 at http://www.transparency.org/cpi2015

Tyler, T. R., & Wakslak, C. J. (2004). Profiling and police legitimacy: Procedural justice, attributions of motive, and acceptance of police authority. *Criminology, 42*(2), 253–282.

Vincentnathan, S. G., & Vincentnathan, L. (2009). The police, community, and community justice institutions in India. In D. Wisler & I. D. Onwudiwe (Eds.), *Community policing: International perspectives and comparative perspectives* (pp. 257–287). Boca Raton: CRC Press.

Zafarullah, H. (2007). Bureaucratic Elitism in Bangladesh: The predominance of generalist administrators. *Asian Journal of Political Science, 15*(2), 161–173.

Chapter 7
Tying It All Together – I'm Smarter than a Ninth Grader – The Culture of Lawfulness Model and Its Origins in the Schools

This author has spent much of the last two decades working on building a model to promote a culture of lawfulness internationally alongside a team under the leadership of Dr. Roy Godson of Georgetown University and the National Strategy Information Center (NSIC). After studying diverse locations around the globe that had successfully overcome decades of entrenched crime and corruption (Palermo, Sicily; Hong Kong, Bogota, Colombia), we distilled some common lessons learned that could be adapted and used to help promote a culture of lawfulness, or a culture that is supportive of the rule of law. Importantly, these lessons recognized that cultural change cannot occur overnight, and can often take over a decade.

Central to building a culture of lawfulness is the recognition of the need to work within all sectors to educate people about the importance of the rule of law, and how each citizen can work to support the rule of law from the different standpoint and perspective of each sector. In sum, the culture of lawfulness model suggests that crime and corruption is never the responsibility of one individual sector, even the police. The multi-sector model builds on what is commonly referred to by some as the public health model or social crime prevention (Grant 2014).

The earliest rule of law education program was piloted in 8 schools in Tijuana, Mexico in the mid-nineties. There, we were approached by a group of secundaria (middle school level) teachers frustrated with the growing involvement of their students in the drug trade as mules, as well as in other forms of crime and corruption. After working with this group to develop and successfully implement a crime prevention curriculum targeting this level, the first culture of lawfulness model was born. Its early successes led to the State of Baja California's support for the expansion of the program statewide where it was subsequently evaluated on a large scale. Further details of this curriculum can be found in Grant (2014).

This chapter is adapted and abridged from Grant. H, J. Grabias, and R. Godson (2006)." The Role of Police in Promoting the Rule of Law'. In *Democratic policing in transitional and developing countries*. Routledge

© The Author(s) 2018
H. B. Grant, *Police Integrity in the Developing World*, SpringerBriefs in Criminology, https://doi.org/10.1007/978-3-030-00413-2_7

Following the statewide evaluation of the program with a sample of over 10,000 students, its success in successfully changing attitudes and beliefs related to the law, rule of law, and obedience towards the law, the program was expanded to two other states in Mexico (Sinaloa and Chihuahua), before going nationwide under the leadership of the federal Secretaria de Educacion Publica. The program continues to reach over a million students a year in Mexico.

The universal appeal and need for these themes in education led to the piloting of the program globally in the United States, Colombia, Peru, El Salvador, Panama, Republic of Georgia, and Mexico. As discussed above, the school-based curriculum was only ever meant to be a tool within a larger multi-sector strategy and not an end in itself. Interestingly, the students in the original (and subsequent) evaluation stressed the need for the police to receive a similar course. In fact, 87% said they would be more likely to support the police if the police upheld the rule of law in their words and actions (Kenney and Godson 2002).

Taking It to the Police

To that end, a police rule of law education program was developed and piloted at the municipal and state levels, before ultimately being piloted currently in the Mexican Federal Police. This police training program was also tested with the federal police in both Colombia and Panama. A central idea in this program focused upon helping participants to see how the police can (and must) contribute to upholding the rule of law.

How can the police foster and sustain support from the community that is fundamental to effective crime prevention and response? Research and experience show the importance of both formal and informal collaboration on crime prevention between various sectors of the community and the police as we have discussed throughout this manuscript (Sherman et al. 1997).

The police have an essential function in a democratic society governed by the rule of law. Part of their role in a rule of law society is, of course, ensuring that no one is above the law, and that individuals or groups do not violently assert their will over the public order. However, police responsibilities extend far beyond this. They are the primary contact that citizens have with government and the justice system. Policing in accordance with the rule of law means that each police officer treats all individuals (both victims and offenders) in accordance with the values that are embodied within the rule of law: fairness, dignity, and respect.

Given their highly visible public place in society, police are central in shaping the attitudes and behavior of others by offering their own actions as examples (Tyler and Huo 2002; Skogan 1990). The police themselves first need to understand what the rule of law is. Given the different educational standards for recruitment internationally, the basic knowledge cannot be taken for granted. Second, for this knowledge to influence their behavior, they have to believe in the ability of the rule of law to improve the quality of life for all members of society. The important role that police can have in shaping community attitudes toward the law has often been documented. Many studies have found that when citizens feel they are likely to be treated fairly by the police, they are also more likely to support the decisions of the police even if the outcome is not to their personal advantage (Tyler 2004; Skogan 1990).

Some may think, "People will not support the police because every time we interact with them we are made to do something that we don't want to do. The police give us traffic tickets, ask us to move along, turn down our music, and so forth." The reality is that if we believe we have been treated with dignity and professionalism by the police officer that gave us the traffic ticket, our attitudes towards the police will not become more negative as result of personal experience.

This same research also indicates that support for the police is directly related to a general willingness to follow the rules and laws of society – in other words, it is related to a culture of lawfulness.

Public support for law enforcement is obviously influenced by high profile cases of police corruption or human rights abuses in the media. However, police routinely taking relatively small bribes, police apathy to citizen concerns, and unprofessional conduct have far greater effects on citizen belief in the rule of law. These are the situations that citizens are most likely to encounter in day-to-day interactions with the police, and have the greatest influence over personal opinions. Police power is not just about the use of force, which typically first comes to mind. The greatest police power derives from their ability to teach others correct behavior by example; to pass on values to society by representing the best that the rule of law has to offer: fairness, justice, and dignity (Caldero and Crank 2004).

A note of caution: most police officers set out with noble intention to "take the bad guys off the streets", respond to victims, and ensure the safety and quality of life of communities. Yet however serious or heinous the crime, engaging in illegal tactics to catch and put in jail a known criminal – planting evidence, subjecting suspects to physical violence, lying in written testimony – can never be justified. Further, such tactics constitute a major threat to the rule of law (Wood 2004; Kleinig 2002). Illegal behavior by police demonstrates to citizens that government can interfere in people's lives with impunity and without regard for the constraints of the rule of law. Although the goal of crime control is essential to the healthy functioning of society, it must be balanced with citizen's right to due process embodied in the rule of law.

Knowledge of the rule of law is merely the foundation for the greater need by the police to believe in its importance, their role in promoting it in the community, and the importance of citizen participation and collaboration. How do we achieve these goals?

Education in the Rule of Law for Police

Rule of law education is designed to equip new or experienced police officers with the knowledge, attitudes, and skills they need to become effective leaders. It aims to help shape police officers who, through their example and their actions, foster widespread societal support for the rule of law – known as the culture of lawfulness. Police, due to the highly visible and sensitive nature of their work, are on the frontline of this effort. They need to act as role models for citizens, demonstrating correct and lawful behavior in the performance of their duties. They also need to act as community leaders in promoting support for rules and law.

Shaping police culture begins in each institution's academic and training programs. Police values are further reinforced on the street by police colleagues, commanders, and through the consistent (or inconsistent) application of the rules and regulations of the institution. Therefore, as a starting point, education about the rule of law and the culture of lawfulness has the potential to promote positive cultural change among the police. More importantly, this kind of education is considered to be a feasible long-term response to the challenges to police effectiveness.

Education in the rule of law is not just about creating better people. It aims to help develop more professional and effective police forces whose every action is based on shared respect for and belief in the principles of the rule of law. Once internalized, these beliefs help shape behavior. As a result, rule of law education also gives police different tools and methods for gaining the trust of citizens that they can use and refine throughout their professional lives.

Rule of law education aims to achieve three goals: convey knowledge, affect, attitudes and build skills. Figure 7.1 demonstrates how these three educational goals work in unison. Each one, on its own, is of useful but limited value. Collectively, however, they contribute to the development of police who, as individuals and officers, value the rule of law and act in ways that uphold it. The foundation of a culture of lawfulness curriculum is building knowledge: therefore, cadets become aware of how their behavior as police can enhance or undermine support for the rule of law, and how citizen support can make policing more effective.

Simultaneously, the program should try to foster attitudes and beliefs in favor of the rule of law and culture of lawfulness. The goal is to encourage cadets to think critically about their identity as police, and why the rule of law is important to their jobs and their dual identities as policeman and citizen. They should believe in the importance of community participation in police work and accept that their role is to help change society and maintain cooperative relationships. A program with the capacity to change the attitudes towards the rule of law is not simply promoting blind obedience to the law or a belief that current societal structures are fine as they are, regardless of the context of corruption, violations of human rights, and so on. Rather, officers should be challenged to think critically about the imperfections that exist within their local context, as well as their own role in influencing closer adherence to the ideal of the rule of law in practice. A major part of this will involve the recognition of how their own actions impact the needed level of citizen support discussed above.

Finally, the program should help cadets put their beliefs into action after graduation from the academy. Given the challenges of responding lawfully and effectively to citizens' needs in dangerous and complex environments, police should be equipped with some basic skills. These include problem solving, critical thinking, legal reasoning, and communication. In the curriculum, participants are confronted

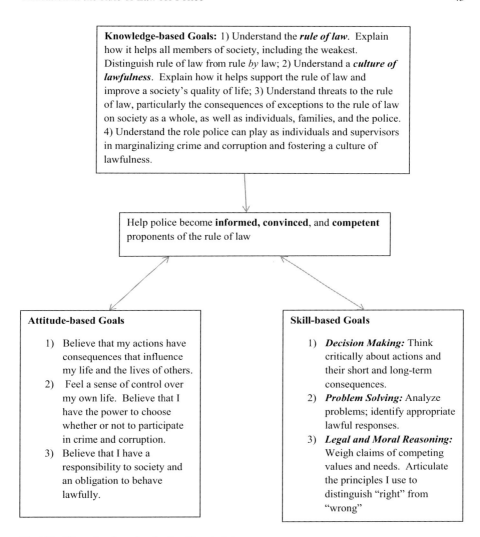

Fig. 7.1 Educational goals of rule of law training

with moral dilemmas based on real-life situations that they may well encounter in the field. Case studies, both positive and negative, will illustrate the benefits – and challenges – of working with the community. Finally, police will be asked to consider some difficult questions that they, their colleagues, or the public might ask: "Why should I be the first one to respect the rule of law? Why shouldn't I take bribes if everyone around me does?"

The interactive methodology of culture of lawfulness education is just as important as the content of the program, as you may have gathered from our discussion in chapter two. Participants, whether they are new cadets or experienced officers, are encouraged to participate actively and critically as much as possible to encourage their evolution into informed, convinced, and competent proponents of the rule of law. In addition, this methodology helps achieve several learning objectives at the same time – participants build skills and attitudes toward the rule of law while also imparting information and knowledge.

A typical rule of law education course for an entry level patrol cadet might cover the following topics; 1) the role of the police in a democracy; 2) the rule of law and a culture of lawfulness (e.g. values, norms, customs, and laws; 4) challenges to effective policing and threats to the rule of law; and 5) promoting a culture of lawfulness in the community. The course is designed to have a practical, concrete effect on cadets' work when they become police. Cadets are expected to gain knowledge, learn skills, and understand the material to the point that it affects their attitudes toward their work. Instructors are prepared to utilize a variety of interactive and dynamic techniques in the classroom (e.g. ethical dilemmas or role playing) to assess cadets' progress in these areas.

Conclusion

What kind of police culture will rule of law education promote? Together, complementary education programs for cadets, in service, and commanders can help foster an organizational culture in which crime and corruption are discouraged, and police are rewarded for upholding and promoting the law. Of course, education does not occur in a vacuum. As discussed throughout this manuscript (and particularly chapters three and four) long-term comprehensive reforms to support the essential foundation of police education. These reforms can include changes to the performance incentives, policies, and especially the processes of recruitment and selection amongst many possibilities. Knowledge, attitudes, and skills need to be supported and reinforced by police supervisors in the field and such institutional mechanisms as those discussed.

It is also important to emphasize as we conclude this manuscript that the police are not responsible for everything as we did in Grant (2014). True, through their job they are tasked with building citizen respect for the rule of law, crime prevention, crime control, and so forth. But promoting a culture of lawfulness – widespread support for the rule of law – is the shared responsibility of all members of society, both government and civil society (Grant 2014; Godson 2000; Orlando 2003; Sherman et al. 1997; Walker 2001). The police are one element of what must be a society wide integrated strategy to improve respect for the rule of law and improve the quality of life for everyone.

Although culture of lawfulness training for police can draw upon the best practices of other countries, it will only be successful to the extent to which it is tailored to and reflects the local contexts of policing within a given society. While part of this will require modifying the types of activities and examples presented in the curriculum, it will also involve providing interactive forums for officers to think critically about local challenges to policing and arrive at possible solutions or proposals for change on their own. This, in turn, must in the long term be supported by larger reforms within the agency and society itself.

Promoting a culture of lawfulness is ultimately about leading by example, both within the police organization and the culture it is embedded in. For the police, values are transmitted from commanding officer to patrolman, patrolman to community. Working together, all can accomplish more. Finally, whether we are talking about organizational or societal change we must also remember that it does not happen overnight, and will require regular reinforcement over even a decade or more.

References

Caldero, M. A., & Crank, J. P. (2004). *Police ethics: The corruption of a noble cause* (2nd ed.). Cincinnati: Anderson.

Godson, R (2000). *A guide to developing a culture of lawfulness* (paper presented at the Symposium on the Role of Civil Society in Countering Organized Crime: Global Implications of the Palermo, Sicily Renaissance), Available at www.unodc.org/palermo/godson.doc.

Grant, H. (2014). *Social crime prevention in the developing world: Exploring the role of police in crime prevention* (Vol. 6). Cham: Springer.

Kenney, D. J., & Godson, R. (2002). Countering crime and corruption: A school-based program on the US-Mexico border. *Criminal Justice, 2*(4), 439–470.

Kleinig, J. (2002). Rethinking noble cause corruption. *International Journal of Police Science & Management, 4*(4), 287–314.

Orlando, L. (2003). Fighting the mafia and renewing Sicilian culture. *Encounter Books.*

Sherman, L. W., Gottfredson, D. C., MacKenzie, D. L., Eck, J., Reuter, P., & Bushway, S. (1997). *Preventing crime: What works, what doesn't, what's promising: A report to the United States Congress.* Washington, DC: US Department of Justice, Office of Justice Programs.

Skogan, W. G. (1990). *Disorder and decline: Crime and the spiral of decay in American cities.* New York: The Free Press.

Tyler, T. R. (2004). Enhancing police legitimacy. *The annals of the American academy of political and social science, 593*(1), 84–99.

Tyler, T. R., & Huo, Y. (2002). *Trust in the law: Encouraging public cooperation with the police and courts through.* New York: Russell Sage Foundation.

Walker, S. (2001). *Police accountability: The role of citizen oversight.* Belmont: Wadsworth Thompson Learning.

Wood, J. (2004). Cultural change in the governance of security. *Policing and Society, 14*(1), 31–48.